The ZEN of TIGGR

by

iGavnali nlaeGai

First Edition

ISBN: 978-1-7948-5302-7

Table of Contents

26 years ago at Kenin-ji temple in Kyoto.

The city of Kyoto had swallowed it up and few Japanese knew what it was or its significance. So I was the only visitor on that day.

I purchased a hand ink drawn BodhiDharma at the little shop.

This was the temple of Eisei who in the 800s traveled to China and brought Zen buddhism to Japan, as BodhiDharma brought it to China from India.

He left the temple to his disciple Myozen. His other disciple, Eihei Dogen Kigen went off to found Eihei-ji temple the foundation of Soto Zen.

I feel so honored to be able to experience such a great place, and saddened that the Japanese have forgotten their own history.

So the story of the photo was realizing the place was empty I told my friend to take my picture in a minute. And then I sat ZaZen. With my perfect mudra. No zafu cushion. But looking now at it my posture and position is just amazing. Perfect. With it I join Dogen and Eisei from 1200 years ago. Same practice. Same awakening. Same livelyhood.

At the time I felt I was so broken and worthless. I wish I could have talked to myself back then. I would have set me straight.

Introduction: Zen and Tiggers

Of course if you are browsing into this title you might know something about ZEN or something about Tiggers. Or you might only know about ZEN or only know about Tiggers. Let me seek to help you out.

ZEN is an odd sort of thing. It itself says we cannot speak about it. So why write books at all.

[puts down the book and scurries off pondering]

[one month later]

Ah ok I think I've got it. Well you see, we write these books for others to enjoy and delight in, and whether you get on or not to truly study ZEN and become a Zen MONK – technically called a BodhiSaatva or one on the Bodhi path – is irrelevant. Bodhi mind or Buddha mind is a special kind of mind "without hindrance" as we learned in the sixth patriarchs sutra. Having some of it I can speak directly about it. It does have its advantages for living and perception.

To a right buddhist, regular folk see the world "as if in a dream" and we scream at them to awaken – GATE GATE PARAGATE

PARASAMGATE- cross cross cross across to the other side. To where you might ask? How very POOH of you I reply.

And that brings us to POOH. Who is probably a very good teacher. This is no mere kids book – the original first text by Milne - "The House at Pooh Corner" - is a remarkable work. There are follow on texts but not much concerning Tigger, a kind of tiger like creature but with a bouncing tail. We can learn a lot by reciting the Tigger song:

The wonderful things about tiggers
Tiggers are wonderful things
Their tops are made out of rubber
Their bottoms are made out of springs
They're bouny flouncy trouncy pouncy
fun fun fun Fun FUN!
But the most wonderful thing about Tiggers is...
I'm the only one. Iiiiiiimmmmm the only one
(growwwwwllllrrrlll)

That is from memory so forgive me if I fit up the trouncy with the poncy I tend to get a bit lost after all these years.

So back to buddhism. Well it came from the buddha, a rich northern indian prince who had never seen the outside world. One day he fled the castle and for the first time saw old people, broken people, hungry people. How can there be so much suffering! And how do I end it! He asked himself. That was the beginning of his quest to find the answer. He tried many teachers and many paths all leading to failure. Finally half starved he received some milk and at that moment had his awakening. Buddhism from that point onwards become a direct transmission of this realization or awakening, from mind to mind, from one to the next, now going on a few thousand years. And they have great lists of who passed to who and different branches of the tree. All very important you know. The part we call ZEN seemed to come up in China around the year 700 and in the year 800-ish a few people made the difficult sea journey from Japan to China, studied in China, ,and brought it back to Japan where it changed from Ch'an to Zen. The japanese not being so good at pronouncing chinese. Lin-Chi a great teacher who told the first koan's or zen stories, well be hecame errr sorry I meant BECAME RINZAI THE GREAT. So one branch was of the RINZAI and thinking on stories. And the stories were collected in things called something like Treasury of the true truth's eye not to be confused with the collection of the not so true truth's nose or some other book.

It seemed to work for a while, but then a lot of people thought maybe this is getting taken a bit too seriously. And that person who crossed over to china – Eisei, well one of his students – Eihei Dogen sometimes called Dogen Kigen which means Dogen with the pointy head, not to be confused with Dogen Maru Atama or Dogen of the round head who didn't look anything like Dogen Kigen, well he went on to get kinda pissed off with the local teachers and left Kenin-ji Temple, a really pretty old place of timbers that I once visited in 1995. The thing about Kenin-ji (ji means temple in japanese) is that the city of Kyoto swallowed it up and instead of being able to sit and meditate the monks got annoyed with the sound of lawn mowers and garbage trucks of their day. So Dogen headed out proclaiming “I shall form a temple where I can finally get some peace” and headed off to remote mountains where he started a place I think it was called DaiButSu-ji which means place without lawn mowers or something like that and later it was renamed Eihei-ji or pointy-head's temple.

Now in the mountains, Dogen could finally think and meditate and wrote quite a few books and they formed into what later become known as the SOTO branch of zen – So meaning noise and TO meaning “not allowed here!”

Well this school was differen't from LinChi's in that they focused more on direct realization of the true nature of the universe before them against a backdrop of what Dogen called U-JI or being time. Kinda like Einstein a thousand years before Einstein. Cool huh?

So instead of focusing on those old dusty books, Dogen showed his students how to do Shikan-Taza or just enough sitting so that they could realize their true nature and see the true universe against a backdrop of eternity. Not easy to explain with words. His other lesser known books - Makura no kebadachi – or the Art of pillow fluffing never quite caught on. You see in zen you sit on rather non fluffy pillows that are round and called Zafu. Finally he got old and smart enough that he didn't really hate the old stories so he decided to gather up the scraps he had and put them together into a book called the Shobogenzo Zuimonki which means dumb stories and scraps I put into a dusty book. But that became his most famous book and actually Dogen didn't even write it

Eihei Dogen Zenji (1200 - 1253)
talks were originally recorded by Koun Ejo Zenji.

So these were direct alive talks. These are called Dharma talks and they are no simple lecture. They are given after the students are sitting in ZAZEN or seated meditation and their minds hopefully refreshed and awake. The talk is the breath of the Dharma (truth) blown into the lazy heads. The thing is, if Dogen had stopped to write it as a book it would have been quite different and without much POWER. So that these are live dharma talks is very important. Shunryu Suzuki had the same thing happen to him in his talks on the Sendokai sutra. One of his students wrote it down and made a book. Ugh. We never quite learn. But in a way it's good because now we get a sense of what Dogen was trying to say to his students, and powerful it was because his lineage became one of the biggest, widest, and most power of all of ZEN producing many great teachers in the process at arriving at today.

So this book, although I have written it down and violated quite so many rules of ZEN which is to be spontaneous, I can assure you it was written with ZEN MIND and as spontaneous as it came to me. Sometimes good, sometimes quite bad. Spelling mistakes and all. And in that approach to writing I think it might obtain something of the POWER OF THE TRUE DHARMA or PawaBoGenZo. But if I titled the book pawabogogenzo who the heck would ever read it. So instead it's the Zen of Tigger. Much less offputting if I do say so myself.

I first caught onto the power in the POOH stories not from the book itself. Although I delighted in Pooh's poems at the time reading it as a kid. No it was one particular episode of the animated series.

In the episode everyone was quite concerned with Eeyore the "sad" depressed donkey. Or so they thought. Eeyore sat on the hill not moving much, and not going to and fro. Others had to go to him, which they thought quite annoying and peculiar. But they did visit him and fill him in as to the goings on in the woods they enlivened. But in this particular episode, when we were all quite certain we understood what Eeyore was all about, some lesson not to be sad and grumpy, for one brief flash at the end, we saw what Eeyore did. And a magnificent brilliant boundless display of nature projected all around him. Eeyore far from being sad, was enlightened. He was seeing the world before him as true direct seeing with no hindrance in the mind under the guise of eternity. At that moment, I had my own Sammadhi or awakening experience and now 40 years later I am writing about it finally in the thinking that someone else may glean some insights from it.

And then it takes us to Tigger. Why is Tigger needed in the story? In the HAPC the characters each fill a role. Christopher Robin is the law giver the top person. You will constantly hear them say "does Christopher Robin" know about this? Kanga is the motherly but a bit worrisome spirit and Roo equates to the beautiful child with "beginners mind" always wanting to try the next new experience life has in store for him, not our old shuttered down minds battered from years of work and cubicles and bosses who tell us we have no value whatsoever. Then there is OWL who complains and thinks nothing will ever succeed. And there is a particularly good chapter when OWLs house gets blown down. And of course we have Pooh himself, a delightful bear who has a good heart but is not always the wisest. Yet somehow, in his seemingly confused state great wisdom comes forth. And that was the basis of the Tao of Pooh as Taoism, a thing like Zen but more chinese and with bigger more pointy hats – is more about free go with the flow and watercourse way. The way that can be spoken of cannot be eaten for breakfast and other wise sayings. Its almost buddhist but definitely not ZEN. So anyhew equating Pooh and Tao is sorta interesting but in this book I try to bring forth how Pooh makes a great advocate for Zen true seeing of the world UNHINDERED in MIND. And perhaps it is Pooh's un-thinking that allows him such astute perceptions. What if something terrible happens asks Piglet? What if it doesn't replies Pooh.

What is the role of Piglet? Pooh's small pig friend? Piglet is like everyday man, quote unquote the rest of us, who seem to always be in a trouble spot or a predicament either Pooh has fallen on top of him or he encounters a huffalump. Life is never easy for Piglet. In later works on the blustery day piglet is swept away by the rains. No the life of a little piglet is always uncertain, Pooh is there to give him a bit of relief. Not to worry so much and enjoy the honey is Poohs lesson to the little guy.

And then Tigger? Tigger is the bodhisaatva on the PATH. He doesn't quite understand everything yet, often gets confused and things wrong as in his encounter with the vicious biting tablecloth yet always goes forth with true spirit and strong heart. Tiggers have several important qualities one of which is that he is the only one. Perhaps recognizing his unique place in the universe is a lesson for all of us. Tiggers also can never be lost. Because they are always precisely where they are. Another good lesson for life.

The HAPC has a dark chapter. And that is Rabbit who is the nemesis of Tigger and seems to hate everything Tigger stands for. While Tigger frolics and has fun Rabbit is busy planting crops. Rabbit is the world of order rules and reason. The world of man. The Lassos that entrap us have deeply entraped Rabbit. And in the dark chapter Rabbit envisions a plan to leave Tigger in the woods LOST. And he convinces everyone that this will be a good lesson for Tigger. Sadly, weakly, the others give in. This is a good lesson for all of us on not giving into the evil plots of rule rigid men. In today's world it reminds me of the double and triple masked people frightened of covid virus. Yet their masks offer no protection at all. Obediently they wear them as marks of shame and disparagement, masks of slavery and obedience. Rabbit meets his Kharmic fate. Kharma is you get what you deserve, you will receive back what you put out in life. And in that poetic justice it is Rabbit that is lost.

In being Lost, and finally found by Tigger Rabbit has an awakening. Rabbit sees Tigger no longer as a menace. Rabbit now sees a big beautiful bouncing Tigger. And rejoices and cries tears of happyness at being finally saved and found. Rabbit cannot understand how Tigger's never get lost yet Rabbits always get lost. So much is behind him and beyond him.

So that is a bit what happens when we do ZEN we live a bit differently and have more of these “special powers” that come from seeing the world truly and not half asleep. It's hard to explain so perhaps the best thing to do at this point is to unleash the real part of this book, the stories or Koans which have two parts. First the EXCERTP from the book and secondly the commentary. Sometimes there is a capping verse. What's that you ask? A capping verse is a final slap across your head to wake you up. Distilled down and made simple and plain or so outrageous you can do nothing but hiccup upon hearing it. I did not always come to a capping verse. But sometimes.

Othertimes the reply contains language and speech-isms that are typical of the old sixth patriarch texts. It's just our tradition to speak that way don't give it much mind.

I hope you enjoy the work and that you will find in it whether an adult or a child or perhaps and hopefully a bit of both a fun path to plod some of your time with smiles and knowing-ness in a way that is more fun that blathering over dusty texts in dark dingy halls or sitting with painful knees in bent up positions reciting silly chants and words.

My books always seem too short compared to the lengthy tomes. But should I say more I will spoil it. It is exactly the length it is. No more no less.

- Gianna giavelli, austin tehaws, november 2021

Prequel. What is a Koan and Lessons of Friendship

One of the things one might ask is what is a koan. And why is this book so weird?

Koan come from the japanese Rinzai sect of Zen Buddhism, the other being SOTO. Interesting enough, Eihei Dogen Kigen was great compiler of Koans. Treasury of the True Dharma Eye or Shobogenzo Zuimonki is one compilation of stories that are much older. These are not so much original writings but rather putting together into a collection. Later my old friend John Daido Loori published the 300 Koan collection.

Koans have a structure. First there is a story. Then there might be a capping verse. Then the commentary.

The capping verse and the commentary is from a zen teacher.

The capping verse literally is to knock you on your head and wake you up to the meaning.

The commentary is to help you with the deeper meaning of what is at work here.

In this book, the stories are stories of Tigger and others from the house at pooh corner book.

One lesson I find in these book, besides the dark plot (where Rabbit seeks to eliminate Tigger altogether by leaving him lost in the woods – How Horrible for a kids book yet... there it is. We tend no to think about how borrible and sorrible that really is but isn't it just dreadful? Rabbit has a change of SPIRIT. This is very important. This is a key lesson in this book. It doesn't quite fit all at once into a koan so it is broken up. How very brave to tell such a dark story of weakness, then despair, then salvation in a "kids book".

The other thing I want to talk about is friendship. These pooh books have a lot of lessons on friendship.

Lets talk about the principal friendship which is Pooh and Piglet. Piglet needs Pooh in many ways. Piglet isn't very big or strong nor really very smart. Pooh one might say is even more troubled in his own special doddering way. A perpetual confusion which actually arises from his unique way to see the world.

Pooh sings his songs and rhymes seeking to always to make some sense of what is going on around him.

The topic of the book is can Pooh and Tigger form a friendship. And what kind of person is Tigger. Is he friendable? He seems to cause trouble and be difficult. Like eating thistles, he might not agree with us so much.

I would argue however, that Tigger is precisely what we hope for in a friend. He is loyal. He has honor. And he approaches the whole world anew all the time in what we in the Zen world call Beginners mind. Our minds get stale. Our minds get cold and dark. To keep them sharp is a large part of what Zen is. So why does Tigger make a great friend? Well for one, he goes ALL IN to every situation. Without reservation. Without effort. And he is always up to the challenges. With him, you'd be on endless adventures and you would find great things and explorations. And it would end with a smile. A Grrrrrooooowl. A trill. That special noise only tiggers make.

Owl is he a good friend? He is a bit formal. And he doesn't really get out into the world much. At best you might get some tea.

Kanga is busy raising Roo and all that entails of motherhood. Eeyore is seemingly depressed (not true!) in his own world not really engaging with the others except for their little talks. And of course Rabbit is so difficult. They all seem to make mistakes that destroy friendships. No principally Piglet is a friend, in a codependent kind of way. But not the best. One marvels ate Piglet and Poo. They somehow make it work like a bad marriage.

Tigger he is the one I would pick to explore the world with. So the lesson for us should be, to be more like Tigger ourselves so that we can explore and be playful.

I went to the grocery and it was xmas eve and was telling everyone merry christmas. I asked a little girl what was her favorite xmas song. In today world she winced back until her father said hello and seemed to accept me as a non threat. And then she talked up a storm. I think our world is too cold and unforgingn and untrustafayin just cause there are so many terrible people in it who would quickly skin you and sell your heart for a buck. That's the sad reality of it.

The lesson of Tigger is not to get so preoccupied with all that. Life won't live itself. Maybe if we were more bouncey, or at least a little bit flouncy, we might capture a bit of the fun fun fun of being... the only one.

I think back to my time in Japan. It does change us to see the great things of the world more so when they are tied to great thoughts and great peoples. I was there in winter. My **Fuubutsushi** – the smells of the fir trees and the misty fogs, falling snow peacefully, the happyness of my time with my love my fiancee throwing snowballs at each other and munching on temple food – big iron pots cooking special fresh tofu and mountain vegetable. Shoes off, shoji screens, the smells of the soy sauce and vegetables aromatizing the air. Or the special 60 taste meal that took four hours with yuzu and concoctions that looks more like special sculptures. The thing about eating in japan is that you are always hungry after as a westerner. I would go out at ten a night and get sticks of rice gluten mush barbequed on a fire and slathered in soy sauce. Doesn't sound good. When you've only eaten sixty tiny bites, it was heaven.

In the mornings we descended and I walked to a corner japanese version of a seven eleven and in a glass box they had heated pre-made cans of coffee with sugar. Ick sugar in coffee! The italian in me was spiteful. But it was all there was there. Each culture achieves perfection in some things but not others. Mine had coffee.

Traveling to Kyoto and being in the shadows of Eisei and Dogen is a powerful thing. Mo no aware. The universe unfolding. My path was already made. The next places were destined to be. Rather than the western concept of hurrying up and arriving there and here, hither and thither scurrying endlessly for money and attainment, Zen slaps you back to smelling the mountain air. A squirrels tail shakes. A crane is standing silently in the pond unnoticed. What does it have to do with living?

To be a buddhist in Kyoto is to be Ukiyo. You see the old wooden everyday buildings standing for 400 years as Geisha and Maiko scurry between running home keeping errands for their Okiya. You are at once lost and living in an old sensibility. Senses of honor pervade.

My fiancee pulls at my sleeve smiling. We accidentally are in front of a very very old Kyoto candy shop selling the traditional candies of Kyoto unchanged since the 1800s. Apparently these mean so much. We go in and buy so many.

The next morning we approach our first BIG temple. Kenin-ji had been enchanting but now we were approaching the famous and impress they did. All along the route to the temple were amazing shops. One was as long as a football field and every six inches was another kind of odd fermented vegetable the likes of which and names for we have not in english. I tried many loving all of them. Daikon with red peppar. Seaweeds which were at once cruncy yet evoked waves. Food as a story. I was amazed.

The past christmas my fiancee had given me a bowl. It was very ornate pottery with thousands of tiny cut out shapes. Of course, I didn't think much of it. I was a bit disappointed really. But there was a pottery shop and it was amazing to see such a traditional building and in myriad tiny windows the pottery each individual piece – a one off – in its own cloister. I walked around inside. The prices were staggering. Five thousand, eight thousand, twenty thousand dollars. The smaller pieces were at least 800. I said nothing but knew immediately that small bowl I had received was a small fortune.

It shows how our values change. And yet intertwine. For me, knowing how to make fresh coppacola or fine pasta or cappucino, for the japanese it was calligraphy, little sweets, tiny decorative pottery, and fermented seaweeds. Buddhism too was one of these gifts from japan but they had just taken it from china and folded it into a very japanesey thing. The Chinese could not complain as they did the same taking it from northern India. Each culture adding. Like a soup of infinite ingredients it became the tastiest and yet indescribable broth. Tigger too struggles trying to understand what he likes to eat best. And the only way to know is to try it all. Thistles. Def NOT what Tiggers like best!

To that end there are lessons for living. A time in our life is for feasting and trying everything, other times for insight, and finally as we enter the slowing years which pass every so quickly each faster than the year before so that it seems we might remain only one second on this earth, well then we have to think about what we add to this eternal golden braid. We can add nothing if we haven't developed our selves nor if we have never suffered, been tortured, abused, starved and struggled. That is the fire that casts our broken parts into a fierce alloy. Blazing, a calm pervades.

We are in the bamboo forest near the temple. They can make anything you can think of out of the bamboo. There are even giant bamboos used to make buildings and bridges. Each trunk can be almost a foot thick. It's not just the outside of the buildings, but holders for scrolls, fans, spoons. If I were to choose the first thing I would plant is bamboo. Then I would want for nothing.

The sun is gently shining through, a big pot is boiling tofu and the vapors exiting a chimney while a rare rabbit scurries through the snow. I take time for my komorebi. I pause. I will not be here soon again. Bathing in the suchness of a special place, I strive to force it deep into my marrow and memories. So that 26 years later I can talk about it today.

The Useless Tree

In the old days of China the warlords would send out armies and destroy the lands, rape the people of all their wealth, and use it as a lesson to make them obey.

Old man Pang had led a simple life. He raised three daughters and fretted that he had no son.

One day the evil soldiers arrived kicking in his door and dragged him out. Show us your wealth, we will take it all from you! They screamed scowling and snarling.

Old man Pang smiled. “I am just an old man in a hut. All I have are these useless trees so twisted they cannot be cut and made into boards. My hut is old and the roof is leaking. And I have not even a son.”

The head soldier spit at the earth. “Leave him, what are we to do steal the dirt!” and so they huffed and puffed off.

“How shall we survive!” weeped the daughters, “We have nothing but useless trees”

A month later the useless trees dropped thousands of almonds onto the ground, and they picked up sacks of them, enough to eat all winter and still more to trade for anything they wanted.

To some people things will seem useless. Their lives will have no value. Everything will be a problem. They will endlessly be in pain and suffering. Remember the story of the useless tree. Sometimes failing is the path to success. Sometimes the best thing you can do is to stop doing.

Japanese words of Insight....

The Japanese always seem to have a more expressive word farm to use to describe complex concepts of being in nature or relations to the world. Here are some of them which are very apropo to HAPC and the zen of Ti double guh err.

Fuubutsushi

"The things – feelings, scents, images – that evoke memories or anticipation for a particular season."

Yellowing leaves for fall, snowy mountain tops for winter, blooming flowers for spring and sunburns for summer.

Ukiyo

"The floating world"

Which refers to living in the moment and being detached from all other bothers in life. Ukiyo-e refers to the japanese wood block prints made famous in the 16 and 1700s.

Komorebi

Bathing in nature. The sun filters through the pine trees and the wind blows gently across the blossoms.

Mo no aware

the japanese word for "the paths of things." It is the awareness of the impermanence of all things and the gentle sadness and wistfulness at their passing. Everything has an order. Everything has a season. The plum blooms before the orange and that before the cantaloupe.

"The bittersweetness of a brief and grading moment of transcendent beauty."

While not a word, this phrase is meant to talk about a heightened appreciation of the beauty in things and evokes a gentle sadness when it goes away, especially since nothing lasts forever.

Zen Words of Insight

Zen also has several words that in a particular way help to understand this complex experience that is the heart of Zen

Prajna Paramita

The great wisdom of the other shore.

Bodhi and especially Bodhi-mind

The buddha way of perceiving as direct seeing the truth

Makyo

the world as illusion

Samsara

The world of endless return, a trap for us

Sammadhi

A little crack into true seeing at first awakening, the mind state of any awakening

U-JI

literally "being-time". For the buddhist it is the space in which time itself unfolds and pulls back just at that moment being pauses or spun forward we get entangled in it. Sub specie aeternis – under the guise of eternity. A point at which great understanding is made clear.

Koan One: Introducing Oneself

"I'm Pooh," said Pooh.

"I'm Tigger," said Tigger.

"Oh!" said Pooh, for he had never seen an animal like this before. "Does Christopher Robin know about you?"

"Of course he does," said Tigger.

Introductions are needed
The tigger is up to the task
who knows of the tigger?
Of course he does

Being positive
lacking nothing
the TiggR does not fear the Pooh

Does Christopher Robin know about you?
Why of course.

Are we not all animals like this?

Koan Two: Only a Quick Codger

"Excuse me a moment, but there's something climbing up your table," and with one loud Worraworraworraworraworra he jumped at the end of the tablecloth, pulled it to the ground, wrapped himself up in it three times, rolled to the other end of the room, and, after a terrible struggle, got his head into the daylight again, and said cheerfully. "Have I won?"

"That's my tablecloth," said Pooh, as he began to unwind Tigger.

"I wondered what it was," said Tigger.

"It goes on the table and you put things on it."

"Then why did it try to bite me when I wasn't looking?"

"I don't think it did," said Pooh.

"It tried," said Tigger, "but I was too quick for it."

When the tablecloth bites
Only a quick codger can survive it
Get your head into daylight
And get back to things

Why did it try to bite me questions TiggR
Surely TiggRs do not taste so good
Pooh waves it off
But Tigger insists in his quickness

Pooh looks on concerned. Tigger feels triumphant!
But the monster vanquished is an illusion
a poor play who struts then vanishes

Capping Verse:
Fearing the terrible struggle
the Tigger emerges unscathed
What was it says the Tigger
He will never quite know
If it's a mere tablecloth
Then why did it try to bite him
Tigger declares it would have were it not for his quickness

Koan Three: Looking at Oneself

When he awoke in the morning, the first thing he saw was Tigger, sitting in front of the glass and looking at himself.

"Hallo!" said Pooh.

"Hallo!" said Tigger. "I've found somebody just like me. I thought I was the only one of them."

The MIRROR the TIGGR where can the dust alight*

Being only one of yourself how can there be two

Falling for the deception, TiggR finds his own friend

Looking past the mirror his stomach growls

- This is a reference to a very important zen story of Hui-Neng the sixth patriarch (or sixth after Bodhidarma, the monk who brought Buddhism from India to China).

Hui neng was a lowly cook at the temple. Rice pounder more exactly he was not the Tenzo or chief cook. No one took much mind of him. And the monk who was to receive the lineage wrote a great poem on the temple wall to show his understand. Here is the story:

After a couple of days, a young monk passed by the kitchen, reciting Shenxiu's poem. As soon as Huineng heard it, he knew it did not express the essence of true nature. Feeling curious, he approached the young monk: "What is this poem you are reciting?"

The young monk looked him over and said: "You are an ignorant barbarian, so of course you would not know. Our Master told us he wished to name his successor, so he ordered us to write a poem to demonstrate our understanding. The one who understands the dharma best will become the Sixth Patriarch. Our teacher Shenxiu wrote his poem on a wall, and the Master told us to recite it. He said if we follow its words in spiritual cultivation, we will reap great benefits."

This made HuiNeng even more curious. He said to the young monk: "I would like to recite it too, but I do not know where the wall is. Can you take me to it, so I can pay my respects?"

The young monk took HuiNeng to the wall. HuiNeng saw the poem, but could not read it because he was illiterate. There was a visitor nearby, a government official by the name of Zhang. He was able to read it out loud for HuiNeng.

> The body is the Bodhi Tree,
> the mind is the stand for a bright mirror -
> at all times diligently polish
> to remain untainted by dust.

Huineng bowed to Zhang: "Sir, I also have a poem. Can you help me write it on the wall?"

Zhang reacted like the young monk, not taking Huineng seriously. He said in a mocking tone: "You know how to write poetry too? Now that would be extremely rare indeed!"

Huineng said calmly: "Those who wish to learn the ultimate teaching should not look down on beginners. The lowest of the low may have the highest wisdom; the highest of the high may have no wisdom. Thus, to look down on someone would be the ultimate wrong."

Zhang was surprised by Huineng's words. He dropped his attitude, and wrote on the wall as Huineng dictated:

> Bodhi has no tree
> Nor a clear mirror nor a stand
> The universe ineffable without a single thing
> Where can the dust alight?

Upon seeing this the temple abbot met with HuiNeng and immediately recognized him as the successor but knowing the other monks would be jealous sent him forth from the temple.

Koan Four: What Do TiggRs Like to Eat?

Tigger took a large mouthful of honey . . . and he looked up at the ceiling with his head on one side, and made exploring noises with his tongue, and considering noises, and what-have-we-got-here noises . . . and then he said in a very decided voice:

"Tiggers don't like honey."

"Oh!" said Pooh, and tried to make it sound Sad and Regretful. "I thought they liked everything."

"Everything except honey," said Tigger.

Pooh felt rather pleased about this, and said that, as soon as he had finished his own breakfast, he would take Tigger round to Piglet's house, and Tigger could try some of Piglet's haycorns.

"Thank you, Pooh," said Tigger, " because haycorns is really what Tiggers like best."

So after breakfast they went round to see Piglet, and Pooh explained as they went that Piglet was a Very Small Animal who didn't like bouncing, and asked Tigger not to be too Bouncy just at first. And Tigger, who had been hiding behind trees and jumping out on Pooh's shadow when it wasn't looking, said that Tiggers were only bouncy before breakfast, and that as soon as they had had a few haycorns they became Quiet and Refined. So by-and-by they knocked at the door of Piglet's house.

"Hallo, Pooh," said Piglet.

"Hallo, Piglet. This is Tigger."

"Oh, is it?" said Piglet, and he edged round to the other side of the table. "I thought Tiggers were smaller than that."

"Not the big ones," said Tigger.

"They like haycorns," said Pooh, "so that's what we've come for, because poor Tigger hasn't had any breakfast yet."

Piglet pushed the bowl of haycorns towards Tigger, and

said, "Help yourself," and then he got close up to Pooh and felt much braver, and said, "So you're Tigger? Well, well!" in a careless sort of voice. But Tigger said nothing because his mouth was full of haycorns....

After a long munching noise he said:

"Ee-ers o i a-ors."

And when Pooh and Piglet said "What?" he said "Skoos ee," and went outside for a moment.

When he came back he said firmly:

"Tiggers don't like haycorns."

"But you said they liked everything except honey," said Pooh.

"Everything except honey and haycorns," explained Tigger.

When he heard this, Pooh said, "Oh, I see!" and Piglet, who was rather glad that Tiggers didn't like haycorns, said, "What about thistles?"

"Thistles," said Tigger, "is what Tiggers like best."

"Then lets go along and see Eeyore," said Piglet

So the three of them went; and after they had walked and walked and walked, they came to the part of the Forest where Eeyore was.

"Hallo, Eeyore!" said Pooh. "This is Tigger."

"What is?" said Eeyore.

"This," explained Pooh and Piglet together, and Tigger smiled his happiest smile and said nothing.

Eeyore walked all round Tigger one way, and then turned and walked all round him the other way.

"What did you say it was?" he asked.

"Tigger."

"Ah!" said Eeyore.

"He's just come," explained Piglet.

"Ah!" said Eeyore again.

He thought for a long time and then said:

"When is he going?"

Pooh explained to Eeyore that Tigger was a great friend of Christopher Robin's, who had come to stay in the Forest, and

Piglet explained to Tigger that he mustn't mind what Eeyore said because he was always gloomy; and Eeyore explained to Piglet that, on the contrary, he was feeling particularly cheerful this morning; and Tigger explained to anybody who was listening that he hadn't had any breakfast yet. I knew there was something," said Pooh. "Tiggers always eat thistles, so that was why we came to see you, Eeyore."

"Don't mention it, Pooh."

"Oh, Eeyore, I didn't mean that I didn't want to see you--"

"Quite--quite. But your new stripy friend-- naturally, he wants his breakfast. What did you say his name was?"

"Tigger."

"Then come this way, Tigger."

Eeyore led the way to the most thistly-looking patch of thistles that ever was, and waved a hoof at it.

"A little patch I was keeping for my birthday," he

said; " but, after all, what are birthdays? Here to-day and gone to-morrow. Help yourself, Tigger."

Tigger thanked him and looked a little anxiously at Pooh.

"Are these really thistles?" he whispered.

"Yes," said Pooh.

"What Tiggers like best?"

"That's right," said Pooh.

"I see," said Tigger.

So he took a large mouthful, and he gave a large crunch.

"Ow!" said Tigger.

He sat down and put his paw in his mouth.

"What's the matter?" asked Pooh.

"Hot!" mumbled Tigger.

"Your friend," said Eeyore, "appears to have bitten on a bee."

Pooh's friend stopped shaking his head to get the prickles out, and explained that Tiggers didn't like thistles.

"Then why bend a perfectly good one?" asked Eeyore.

"But you said," began Pooh, "--you said that Tiggers liked everything except honey and haycorns."

"And thistles," said Tigger, who was now running round in circles with his tongue hanging out.

Running in circles
The thistles make him dance
Not honey not haycorns not thistles
What can a TiggR eat?

TiggRs like to eat everything of course
when every-thing is not honey nor haycorns nor thistles
Dejected, the prickles pounce
Live not with your tongue hanging out
The food you like is just around the next corner

What shall we do about poor little TiggR
if he eats nothing he'll never get bigger
Untrained untrue the true source shines through

The capping verse:
bumbling along it takes some time to find our true nature
when we do it will be like gulps of delicious syrup
then we have found our true home
and the rest of our living can truly begin

Koan Five: Let Things Come

"He's quite big enough anyhow," said Piglet.

"He isn't really very big."

"Well he seems so."

Pooh was thoughtful when he heard this, and then he murmured to himself:

But whatever his weight in pounds, shillings,
and ounces,
He always seems bigger because of his bounces.

"And that's the whole poem," he said. "Do you like it, Piglet?"

"All except the shillings," said Piglet. "I don't think they ought to be there."

"They wanted to come in after the pounds," explained Pooh, " so I let them. It is the best way to write poetry, letting things come."

Seeming bigger, bouncing is not for the weak codger
A moon could tell it!
Let things come as they need to
To form a true whole

Shillings always sit between pounds and ounces
were they not there would you sense the emptyness?
Everything comes in just the right order
That is the

The capping verse:
what do we truly see?
Is it bigger or very big
being thoughtful, the question is withdrawn

Koan Six: Being Strengthened Quite Enough!

"What is it?" whispered Tigger to Piglet.

"His Strengthening Medicine," said Piglet. "He hates it."

So Tigger came closer, and he leant over the back of Roo's chair, and suddenly he put out his tongue, and took one large gololLop, and, with a sudden jump of surprise, Kanga said, "Oh!" and then clutched at the spoon again just as it was disappearing, and pulled it safely back out of Tigger's mouth. But the Extract of Malt had gone.

"Tigger dear!" said Kanga.

"He's taken my medicine, he's taken my medicine, he's taken my medicine!" sang Roo happily, thinking it was a tremendous joke.

Then Tigger looked up at the ceiling, and closed his eyes, and his tongue went round and round his chops, in case he had left any outside, and a peaceful smile came over his face as he said, "So that's what Tiggers like!"

Which explains why he always lived at Kanga's house afterwards, and had Extract of Malt for breakfast, dinner, and tea. And sometimes, when Kanga thought he wanted strengthening, he had a spoonful or two of Roosbreakfast after meals as medicine.

"But I think," said Piglet to Pooh, "that he's been strengthened quite enough."

When you find the true source
you have it for breakfast lunch and dinner
Move into that house and never leave
How could TiggR get strengthened more?

Finding what TiggRs like
is like finding your family
a stodgy blind man could see it
Why is piglet disdainful?

Wrestling the spoon from the hand
the malt hits the mouth
how delicious
what has been missing all along is already there

smiling peacefully
at once the TiggR knows
a truth beyond words
the taste of the wonderful spoon

Koan Seven: Not Meaning to be Underneath

"Pooh!" squeaked the voice.

"It's Piglet!" cried Pooh eagerly. "Where are you?"

"Underneath," said Piglet in an underneath sort of way.

"Underneath what?"

"You," squeaked Piglet. "Get up!"

"Oh!" said Pooh, and scrambled up as quickly as he could. "Did I fall on you, Piglet?"

"You fell on me," said Piglet, feeling himself all over.

"I didn't mean to," said Pooh sorrowfully.

"I didn't mean to be underneath," said Piglet sadly.

Where we are
above or underneath
like the foot before and after in walking
Underneath what is the capping question
not meaning to stray, the Piglet lies underneath

Did I fall on you? Then what am I
Where are you beneath the sky
above or underneath
scramble up quickly

The piglet does not complain
but commands directly
GET UP
and the question remains
Underneath WHAT?
You comes the reply

Koan Eight: Trapping a Huffalump

PIGLET (surprised): "Hullo! This is a trap I've made, and I'm waiting for a Heffalump to fall into it."

HEFFALUMP (greatly disappointed): "Oh!" (After a long silence): "Are you sure?"

PIGLET: "Yes."

HEFFALUMP: "Oh!" (nervously): "I--I thought it was a trap I'd made to catch Piglets."

PIGLET (surprised): "Oh, no!"

HEFFALUMP: "Oh!" (Apologetically): "I--I must have got it wrong then."

PIGLET: "I'm afraid so." (Politely): "I'm sorry." (He goes on humming.)

HEFFALUMP: "Well-well-I-well. I suppose I'd better be getting back?"

PIGLET (looking up carelessly): "Must you? Well, if you see Christopher Robin anywhere, you might tell him I want him."

HEFFALUMP (eager to please): "Certainly! Certainly!"
(He hurries off.)

Getting it wrong is the first step in the path
Seeing Huffalumps without seeing them
Piglet protests the leaving
Maybe the hole was not big enough?

Does the Huffalump catch the Piglet
or does the Piglet catch the Huffalump
A moment of yes and no
Lost is your soul

If you seek the Huffalump
First learn to recognize its tracks

Koan Nine: What are you looking for?

And two days later Rabbit happened to meet Eeyore in the Forest.

"Hallo, Eeyore," he said, "what are you looking for?"

"Small, of course," said Eeyore. "Haven't you any brain?"

"Oh, but didn't I tell you?" said Rabbit. "Small was found two days ago."

There was a moment's silence.

"Ha-ha," said Eeyore bitterly. "Merriment and what-not. Don't apologize. It's just what would happen."

Eeyore has been forgotten again
He wanders pointedly
Small is not there
How can he find the found?

Things are just what would happen
how could they be anything else
no apology is needed
one would sooner apologize for the sky

Sometimes not having a brain and wandering is the best path
Lest one lose the chase
Merriment and what-not
says the proud one
It's never too late

Koan Ten: Not Mattering What you do

I could spend a happy morning
Seeing Roo,
I could spend a happy morning
Being Pooh.
For it doesn't seem to matter,
If I don't get any fatter
(And I don't get any fatter),
What I do.

If we spend just one morning being oneself
how can we not be happy?
Not mattering is a smattering
a fattering of what I do?

No says the Pooh
not mattering what I do is
the most mattering you can do
whether seeing Roo
or Being Pooh
not mattering is what I do

Can you grasp it?
The sound of an acorn cracking in the woods
Is the outside in or the inside through?
The path is not what matters
All that matters is being you

Koan Eleven: Whatever we want to be in time for

And as they went, Tigger told Roo (who wanted to know) all about the things that Tiggers could do.

"Can they fly?" asked Roo.

"Yes," said Tigger, "they're very good flyers, Tiggers are. Strornry good flyers."

"Oo!" said Roo. "Can they fly as well as Owl?"

"Yes," said Tigger. "Only they don't want to."

"Why don't they want to?" well, they just don't like it somehow."

Roo couldn't understand this, because he thought it would be lovely to be able to fly, but Tigger said it was difficult to explain to anybody who wasn't a Tigger himself.

"Well," said Roo, "can they jump as far as Kangas?"

"Yes," said Tigger. "When they want to."

"I love jumping," said Roo. "Let's see who can jump farthest, you or me."

"I can," said Tigger. "But we mustn't stop now, or we shall be late."

"Late for what?"

"For whatever we want to be in time for," said Tigger, hurrying on.

Not stopping not resting

A TiggR cannot be late

Mustn't stop now

Or we won't arrive at our fate

Jumping the furthest

Or Bouncing the highest

The TiggR avoids all tests

Knowing he is the best

Sometimes all that matters is moving forward

To stop would be quick and painless

the wise sage bounds onwards

Does the TiggR fall to the test

Roo is always trying to measure

But the best things

Cannot be

Koan Twelve: Feeling Singy, The Fir Tree Slips Away

One day, when Pooh was walking towards this bridge, he was trying to make up a piece of poetry about fir-cones, because there they were, lying about on each side of him, and he felt singy. So he picked a fir-cone up, and looked at it, and said to himself, "This is a very good fir-cone, and something ought to rhyme to it." But he couldn't think of anything. And then this came into his head suddenly:

Here is a myst'ry
About a little fir-tree.
Owl says it's his tree,
And Kanga says it's her tree.

"Which doesn't make sense," said Pooh, "because Kanga doesn't live in a tree."

He had just come to the bridge; and not looking where he was going, he tripped over something, and the fir-cone

jerked out of his paw into the river.
"Bother," said Pooh, as it floated slowly under the
bridge, and he went back to get another fir-cone which had a
rhyme to it. But then he thought that he would just look at the
river instead, because it was a peaceful sort of day, so he lay
down and looked at it, and it slipped slowly away beneath him .
. . and suddenly, there was his fir-cone slipping away too.

Who owns the fir tree
Does making it your home work for it
Watch where you step
or it will slip through your fingers

Not looking not seeing
Pooh enters the true space
Not grasping or thinking
The fir tree slips away

A bodhisaatva would be proud
In a moment of yes and no
the fir-cone and the fir-tree are one
Distracted by the river
who owns what fades away

Koan Thirteen: Swimming Round and Round is much more difficult

"Yes, because it's grey. A big grey one. Here it comes!
A very--big--grey---- Oh, no, it isn't, it's Eeyore."

And out floated Eeyore.

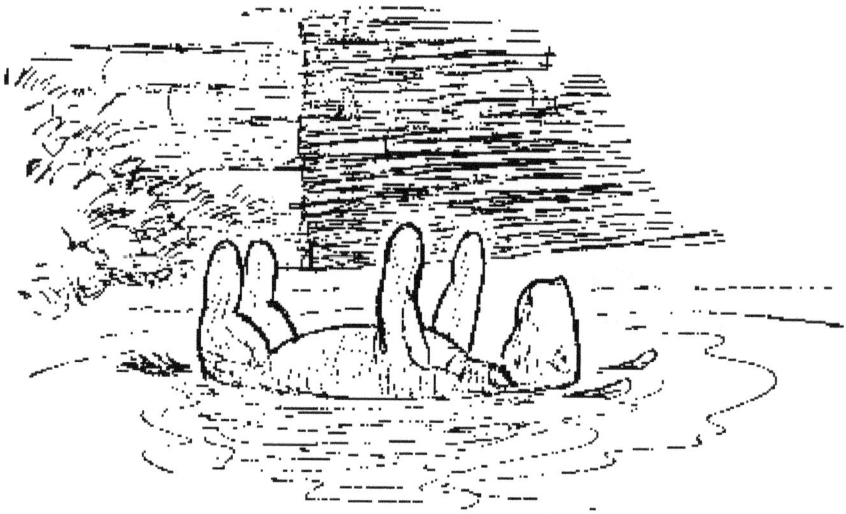

"Eeyore!" cried everybody.

Looking very calm, very dignified, with his legs in the air, came Eeyore from beneath the bridge.

"It's Eeyore!" cried Roo, terribly excited.

"Is that so?" said Eeyore, getting caught up by a little eddy, and turning slowly round three times. "I wondered."

"I didn't know you were playing," said Roo.

"I'm not," said Eeyore.

"Eeyore, what are you doing there?" said Rabbit.

"I'll give you three guesses, Rabbit. Digging holes in the ground? Wrong. Leaping from branch to branch of a young oak-tree? Wrong. Waiting for somebody to help me out of the river? Right. Give Rabbit time, and he'll always get the answer."

"But, Eeyore," said Pooh in distress, "what can we--I mean, how shall we--do you think if we--"

"Yes," said Eeyore. "One of those would be just the thing. Thank you, Pooh."

"He's going round and round," said Roo, much impressed.

"And why not?" said Eeyore coldly.

"I can swim too," said Roo proudly.
"Not round and round," said Eeyore. "It's much more difficult.

Mistaken for a stick
Eeyore spinds round and round
harder than swimming
Roo is confounded

Questioned about playing
the sage replies assuredly he is not
this is a more serious game
than stick hunting spot

What is he doing there? Three guesses
He is being a saint to feed them their honey

just at it occurs to him
he comes to practice going round and round
is that not better than wasting a day swimming?

Koan Fourteen: All the possibilities...

"When I want to be washed, Pooh, I'll let you know."

"Supposing we hit him by mistake?" said Piglet anxiously.

"Or supposing you missed him by mistake," said Eeyore.
"Think of all the possibilities, Piglet, before you settle down to enjoy yourselves."

Being hit by mistake is not as sad a fate
as forgetting all the possibilities
Eeyore disarms them before the plan is commenced
When he is ready to be washed he will tell them
not a second before

Eeyore is wise to remind them
of the biggest mistake of all
is not to think of all the possibilities

here is the capping verse:
  deep in the river
  how to get to the other side
  throw a big stone
  and upon the waves ride
  he surrenders the possibility before thinking
  and fails in the task

Koan Fifteen: All the same at the bottom of a river

"How did you fall in, Eeyore?" asked Rabbit, as he dried him with Piglet's handkerchief.

"I didn't," said Eeyore.

"But how--"

"I was BOUNCED," said Eeyore.

"Oo," said Roo excitedly, "did somebody push you?"

"Somebody BOUNCED me. I was just thinking by the side of the river--thinking, if any of you know what that means--when I received a loud BOUNCE."

"Oh, Eeyore!" said everybody.

"Are you sure you didn't slip?" asked Rabbit wisely.

"Of course I slipped. If you're standing on the slippery bank of a river, and somebody BOUNCES you loudly from behind, you slip. What did you think I did?"

"But who did it?" asked Roo.

Eeyore didn't answer.

"I expect it was Tigger," said Piglet nervously.

"But, Eeyore," said Pooh, "was it a Joke, or an Accident? I mean--"

"I didn't stop to ask, Pooh. Even at the very bottom of the river I didn't stop to say to myself, 'Is this a Hearty Joke, or is it the Merest Accident?' I just floated to the surface, and said to myself, 'It's wet.' If you know what I mean."

"And where was Tigger?" asked Rabbit.

Before Eeyore could answer, there was a loud noise behind them, and through the hedge came Tigger himself.

"Hallo, everybody," said Tigger cheerfully.

"Hallo, Tigger," said Roo.

Rabbit became very important suddenly.

"Tigger," he said solemnly, "what happened just now?"

"Just when?" said Tigger a little uncomfortably.

"When you bounced Eeyore into the river."

"I didn't bounce him."

"You bounced me," said Eeyore gruffly.

"I didn't really. I had a cough, and I happened to be behind Eeyore, and I said 'Grrrr--oppp--ptschschschz.'"

"Why?" said Rabbit, helping Piglet up, and dusting him. "It's all right, Piglet."

"It took me by surprise," said Piglet nervously.

"That's what I call bouncing," said Eeyore. "Taking people by surprise. Very unpleasant habit. I don't mind Tigger being in the Forest," he went on, "because it's a large Forest, and there's plenty of room to bounce in it. But I don't see why he should come into my little corner of it, and bounce there. It isn't as if there was anything very wonderful about my little corner. Of course for people who like cold, wet, ugly bits it is something rather special, but otherwise it's just a corner, and if anybody feels bouncy "

"I didn't bounce, I coughed," said Tigger crossly.

"Bouncy or coffy, it's all the same at the bottom of the river."

Joke or accident
all that matters is being wet
taking people by surprise is unpleasant business

What happened just now?
Just When? Replied the TiggR
Before you answer now is behind you!
TiggR will not fall for the first trap

Bouncyness and Coffyness are one and the same
The two branches split in mid stream
No difference no separation is to be found
at the bottom of the river

Koan Sixteen: the sound of one paw clapping

"He just is bouncy," said Piglet, "and he can't help it."

"Try bouncing me, Tigger," said Roo eagerly. "Eeyore, Tigger's going to try me. Piglet, do you think--"

"Yes, yes," said Rabbit, "we don't all want to speak at once. The point is, what does Christopher Robin think about it?"

"All I did was I coughed," said Tigger.

"He bounced," said Eeyore.

"Well, I sort of boffed," said Tigger.

"Hush!" said Rabbit, holding up his paw

There can be no critique being one's own true dharma
The nature is fixed a duck swims a bird flies the bouncing is built in
Rabbit appeals to authority on the matter
Tigger pleads the middle path – neither bouncing nor coughing perhaps it was a boff?

Rabbit has grasped the true nature and holds up a paw
TiggR smiles
Only he understands the message

Not speaking at once how can we defend the thief in the night?
Bouncing and coughing are two arrows meeting in mid air
Separate the bounce from the tiggR and what remains there?

Koan Seventeen: on not being sad

"I should hate him to go on being Sad," said Piglet doubtfully.

"Tiggers never go on being Sad," explained Rabbit. "They get over it with Astonishing Rapidity. I asked Owl, just to make sure, and he said that that's what they always get over it with. But if we can make Tigger feel Small and Sad just for five minutes, we shall have done a good deed."

"Would Christopher Robin think so?" asked Piglet.

"Yes," said Rabbit. "He'd say 'You've done a good deed,

Rabbit is setting the trap will they fall for it?
Never go on being sad is not the game at hand
Piglet raises the alarm and appeals to Christopher Robin
But the Rabbit is having none of it

Calling the trap a good deed
Does it matter if a tiggR stays sad
The moon weeps in its own reflection

Making the TiggR feel small
will that not end his bouncing
A star streaks across the sky
like a tear down the tiggRs cheek

selling the deed as good
Rabbit smiles to himself
satisfied, the plan moves forward
is it not always such within the hearts of men?

Koan Eighteen: Not looking for it, it is found

"How would it be," said Pooh slowly, "if, as soon as we're out of sight of this Pit, we try to find it again?"

"What's the good of that?" said Rabbit.

"Well," said Pooh, "we keep looking for Home and not finding it, so I thought that if we looked for this Pit, we'd be sure not to find it, which would be a Good Thing, because then we might find something that we weren't looking for, which might be just what we were looking for, really."

"I don't see much sense in that," said Rabbit.

"No," said Pooh humbly, "there isn't. But there was going to be when I began it. It's just that something happened to it on the way."

"If I walked away from this Pit, and then walked back to it, of course I should find it."

"Well, I thought perhaps you wouldn't," said Pooh. "I just thought."

Seeking Not Finding
Not Finding is the true seeking
Returning to the lost point
brings you home

Rabbit cannot see the sense it it
And Pooh declares there cannot be
There at the beginning not there at the end
what's the good of that?

Pooh admits he knew Rabbit could not see it
but he proffers forward regardless

Will reason lead you out of the pit
Only anti-reason will get you there
In his stomach Pooh knows this to be true
But Rabbit will never be convinced

Koan Nineteen: Once pushed away, Happy to see again

So he went home with Pooh, and watched him for quite a long time... and all the time he was watching, Tigger was tearing round the Forest making loud yapping noises for Rabbit. And at last a very Small and Sorry Rabbit heard him. And the Small and Sorry Rabbit rushed through the mist at the noise, and it suddenly turned into Tigger; a friendly Tigger, a Grand Tigger, a Large and Helpful Tigger, a Tigger who bounced, if he bounced at all, in just the beautiful way a Tigger ought to bounce.

"Oh, Tigger, I am glad to see you," cried Rabbit.

The despised one is welcomed
Even with bouncing
TiggR becomes ever larger in Rabbit's sad eyes
the Grand TiggR arrives

Bouncing just as he ought to
Rabbit no longer feels scorn
Even the most angry man welcomes the buddha in
when alone and hungry in the woods

The Bounce, the TiggR nature
just as it ought to be
Clear seeing for the first time
Rabbit has no gripe

Koan Twenty: A reason for Go-ing

"Let's go and see everybody," said Pooh. "Because when you've been walking in the wind for miles, and you suddenly go into somebody's house, and he says, 'Hallo, Pooh, you're just in time for a little smackerel of something,' and you are, then it's what I call a Friendly Day."

Piglet thought that they ought to have a Reason for going to see everybody, like Looking for Small or Organizing an Expotition, if Pooh could think of something

Pooh could.

"We'll go because it's Thursday," he said, "and we'll go to wish everybody a Very Happy Thursday. Come on, Piglet."

Smackerels of something abound
after walking in the wind for miles
why need a reason?

Piglet is concerned
Things need reasons to do them
How can he be acquited?

Pooh has the answer
Go because it is thursday
As good as any answer

The capping verse:

going not going
what reason is needed
when smackerels abound?
A wise man can organize a thousand expotitions
and still not get it

Koan TwentyOne: Supposing a Tree

The wind was against them now, and Piglet's ears streamed behind him like banners as he fought his way along, and it seemed hours before he got them into the shelter of the Hundred Acre Wood and they stood up straight again, to listen, a little nervously, to the roaring of the gale among the tree-tops. '

"Supposing a tree fell down, Pooh, when we were underneath it?"

"Supposing it didn't," said Pooh after careful thought.

Supposing not supposing
still the tree falls down
the gale roars unabated

Piglets concern is answered
Supposing it didn't
Pooh understands the forrest

a fool looks for falling trees
and changes his path
a wise man continues forward

Koan TwentyTwo: Not Having Tea

"Pooh," said Piglet nervously.

"Yes?" said one of the chairs.

"Where are we?"

"I'm not quite sure," said the chair.

"Are we--are we in Owl's House?"

"I think so, because we were just going to have tea,
and we hadn't had it."

Supposing not supposing

If no tea is served
How can you have arrived
Pooh looks at his empty cup

Being where you are
is as simple as having tea
no reason to get nervous

Koan TwentyThree: Nothing Particular

I lay on my chest
And I thought it best
To pretend I was having an evening rest;
I lay on my tum
And I tried to hum
But nothing particular seemed to come.
My face was flat
On the floor, and that
Is all very well for an acrobat;
But it doesn't seem fair
To a Friendly Bear
To stiffen him out with a basket-chair
And a sort of sqoze
Which grows and grows
Is not too nice for his poor old nose,
And a sort of squch
Is much too much
For his neck and his mouth and his ears and
such

The rest is pretended and the mind cannot sleep

Flat on the floor is no way for non-acrobats

Still, at a loss, why nothing particular comes?

Perhaps nothing particular coming is the better than something not-particular. Not particular and particular which is the wiser action? An old bear growls.

The codger continues his word games

Speaking of Sqoze is the least of it

why pretend to rest

Koan TwentyFour: There is always hope

For lo! the wind was blusterous
And flattened out his favourite tree;
And things looked bad for him and we--
Looked bad, I mean, for he and us--
I've never known them wuss

Then Piglet (PIGLET) thought a thing
"Courage!" he said "There's always hope
I want a thinnish piece of rope
Or, if there isn't any, bring
A thickish piece of string"

Having courage there is always hope
thinking a thing Piglet knows no wuss
thicker or thinner, a string will suffice
flattened trees will walk again upright

Winds are always blusterous
Life does not wait
Houses blown down
Making no sound
Piglet shows courage to take the right action
it matters not how thick the string

Koan TwentyFive: no exchange of thought ... things must come and go

"No Give and Take," Eeyore went on. "No Exchange of Thought. 'Hallo--What'-- I mean, it gets you nowhere, particularly if the other person's tail is only just in sight for the second half of the conversation."

"It's your fault, Eeyore. You've never been to see any of us. You just stay here in this one corner of the Forest waiting for the others to come to you. Why don't you go to them sometimes?"

Eeyore was silent for a little while, thinking.

"There may be something in what you say, Rabbit," he said at last. "I have been neglecting you. I must move about more. I must come and go."

Eeyore spots it plainly

no exchange can occur

tails are never in sight

at the end

being silent, the truth comes to him at last

the great neglect appears

being at rest will not suffice

only coming and going leaves him without fault

Koan TwentySix: Never heard of before

"There are seven verses in it."

"Seven?" said Piglet as carelessly as he could. "You don't often get seven verses in a Hum, do you, Pooh?"

"Never," said Pooh. "I don't suppose it's ever been heard of before."

Pooh hears the unheard

Seven why not eight?

Piglet gets careless to hit the codger on the head

hearing the unheard of

seven is far too much

still, now it is too late

Koan TwentySeven: thought I ought

Those two bothers will have
   to rhyme with each other
      Buther
   The fact is this is more difficult
            than I thought,
            I ought--
            (Very good indeed)
            I ought
            To begin again,
            But it is easier
            To stop
            Christopher Robin, good-
bye
            I
            (Good)
            I
            And all your friends
            Sends--
            I mean all your friend
            Send--
        (Very awkward this, it keeps
            going wrong)
            Well, anyhow, we send
            Our love
            END

A poem keeps going wrong

the final pooh song

Two bothers rhyme with buther

How could there be another

Struggling to compose the capping verse

The rhymes are unfolding and getting worse

A very awkward bit at first

puts our poor friend into a fit

Until he grasps the import of his verse

“we send our love”

“the end”

is grand discourse

Eeyore tell us

it comes from his quiet moment

when he sat alone on the hill

they feared he was sad and alone

but he was gazing into eternity

Wrapping Things Up – Live Your Favorite Day

"What day is it?"
"It's today,"
squeaked Piglet.
"My favorite day,"
said Pooh.

We have come to the end dear reader. But before I let you go I wanted to beseech you to ponder one thing. You were not here for millions and billions of years. Then you were here. Then you will not be here again for millions and billions of years. So what will you do with today?

I have a sort of test I use to guide me. If what I do doesn't matter in 500 years I don't do it. Unless its food health basic shelter. For example, I have many great ideas to write about the great covid flu of 2021. But, that is an event that has come, will be gone, and be of little use to people in 2521. So should I invest in that? Or some software I might write. Totally forgotten and non-existent in 10 years. It doesn't seem like that is the right path. What you invest your life in is important. The first goal should be freedom, as much as possible, from the enslavers who wish to suck all your life away in exchange for a few bucks. Easier said than done I know. The system is created to do that and it is PERFECTED.

But with great resolution and effort you might find your way to "right livelyhood" I've not quite reached that me-self. But almost.

But even with accomplishments that might reverberate and teach and last 500 years, surely they fade to useless in the gaze of a billion years. What then?

There must be a second side to living. And that is as simple as enjoying the day. Make your day your favorite day. I particularly like buttermilk pancakes made with real fresh buttermilk. But I'm allergic to wheat, gluten, and phytates. I've tried over and over and nothing suffices except the real stuff. So some days I just go ok, but when I eat those pancakes I will cherish and enjoy and experience every last depth that I can perceive of them. And as its no fun to go slow, I devour them hungrily. And I will remember them.

I think life must be like this. We make our choices, we weave our impossible bargains with ourselves, and then we proceed to devour it hungrily. If you are sad, wasting away in a dark corner you don't understand anything at all. If you are simply trying to build accomplishment and proving something or gaining wealth go go go drive drive work harder harder harder then you still don't have it.

I think of my sister working late on christmas eve. They have promised her a retirement if only she gives them her entire life until she is 55. Maybe a fair trade. Maybe.

Your life is always going to be too short to start in old age. And in youth we are soo lost and confused. If you are lucky you had a loving family as a edifice to fall back on. But most don't. Mostly it can be a lot of shit and horror.

How can you make today your favorite day. If you've sacrificed day after day after day doing what they said you needed to do, take today for yourself. Plan a favorite day. What would that be for you? Enjoy it like Pooh before a large vat of honey there can be no excess. Sure you might have nightmarish dreams of woozles, but in the end we survive. Life is about stout stuff, adventures, climbing pyramids and being a bit crazy. No one every looked back at age 80 on the safe and predictable path and though Oh that's what I was supposed to do I have succeeded. No instead – why is life so empty. You have to fill your life up. Whether that's going down the nile river in a raft with cannibals or finding a village in the himalaya with green pastures and beautiful women. Who knows? The only thing we do now is each year we get older and slower and a bit more crotechetly and some even bitter. Zen tells us to awaken to our original powerful mind. Something we once knew but now have lost. If you are dreaming then you might never come out of the dream. That is the way today. A million contrivences and a million things that must be done each day or else... or else WHAT? Really what could happen? One day I was working in a terrible place. I was pretty young still. My boss was an ass. The four of us gathered together. It was still early in the morning, we had all checked in, made the rounds. People knew we were there. "Let's go to the beach!" I chimed. "whaaaa?" But slowly their looks of astonishment changed to smiles. And unabashedly we then left, headed for a most glorious day at the beach, seafood, salt and sea fresh air. We got back at the end of the day and went back to our work a day lives. No one had noticed.

If you live today as your favorite day, then when you are old and sick in your bed you can remember all your favorite days and never feel like you left an ounce of juice in that orange called life. Drain it all and do what must be done.

Zen is a curious thing. No books. No bible. No words that express it. To know it is to be awake and alive. It is as simple as that.

We call it to see the world under the guise of eternity. Seeing our life as if we fall away and time speeds up at the end of time. It isn't about accomplishment or giving great merit. When the emporer met bodhi dharma he asking him – I have built many great temples, what merit have I? And Bodhi Dharma replied none whatsoever. The sacred is not about pleasing or scoring in some odd game.

One reason I like the Pooh stories is that things are always a trouble, a bother, a difficulty. Yet still, they overcome and have adventures in the midst of it. If you lose your sense of that, then you cannot be helped.

The average person is in a sad state really. Knowing almost nothing and pushed on with a million requirements. This modern world is quite odd really compared to the man in the cave who takes out his pole and brings in a fish, pulls up his pot and has an octopus. Life was simpler. We have not evolved for this go go eat the world pace. Dial it all back and thrust out the distractions and sounds. Remember the pointy headed one needed to get away from it all also.

There will be plenty of time to work hard and gain merit and fortune. Take today for yourself. It will be one of your favorite days.

www.ingramcontent.com/pod-product-compliance
Lightning Source LLC
Chambersburg PA
CBHW052154050325
23058CB00003B/38
* 9 7 8 1 7 9 4 8 5 3 0 2 7 *